THE GREASE ALBUM

an armand eisen/thomas durwood publication

Ariel ✦✦ Books

distributed by Ballantine Books

Edited by Armand Eisen   Written by Michael Sollars

THE GREASE ALBUM

Cover photo and photo on page 16 by Alan Pappé/Lee Gross Associates, Inc.

Special thanks to Richard Weston and Howard Levine of Paramount Pictures Corporation. Special thanks also to Arthur T. Birsh of Playbill.

Library of Congress Catalogue Number 78-67280   ISBN 0-345-27887-9

Manufactured in U.S.A.
First Edition: August, 1978

Associate Editor, Michael Sollars

DIDI CONN

DINAH MANOFF

STOCKARD CHANNING

JAMIE DONNELLY

JOHN TRAVOLTA

EVE ARDEN

DODY GOODMAN

FRANKIE AVALON

JEFF CONAWAY

BARRY PEARL

MICHAEL TUCCI

OLIVIA NEWTON-JOHN

KELLY WARD

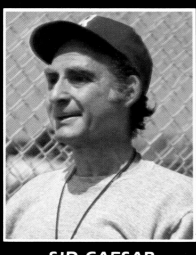

SID CAESAR

ALICE GHOSTLEY

EDD BYRNES

PLAYBILL

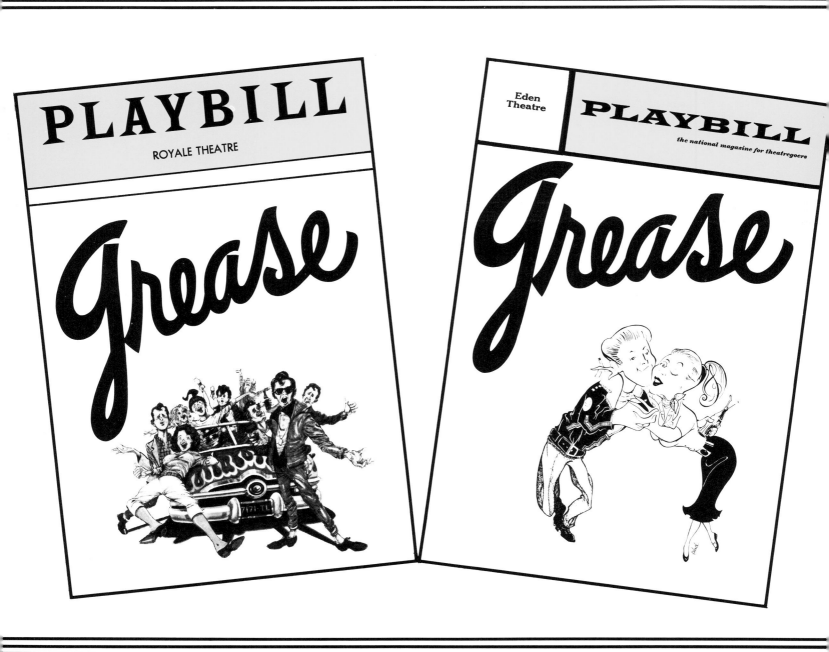

Broadway

Grease Alumni

Grease is known as the toughest show on Broadway to audition for, say producers Kenneth Waissman and Maxine Fox. "Our standards are very high," states Ken. "For each company of *Grease* we put together, director Tom Moore, choreographer Patricia Birch, Maxine and I audition an average of 2,000 actors and actresses to find the 16 freshest and most versatile people around. Each one has to be an excellent actor and singer, and also a fairly good dancer. So it's no accident that network executives are waiting in the wings, ready to swoop up our discoveries as soon as their contracts expire."

The first *Grease* "find" to be tapped for TV stardom was Adrienne Barbeau, who originated the role of Rizzo — the tough leader of the "Pink Ladies" gang in the original Broadway company. Today, Miss Barbeau is known to millions of TV fans as Carol on the "Maude" series.

The most sensational example of the kind of success *Grease* has spawned is John Travolta, the new teenage idol who plays Vinnie Barbarino on "Welcome Back, Kotter." Travolta receives more fan mail than his TV rival "The Fonz" and has been the subject of cover stories for *TV Guide, Celebrity, Playgirl* and *People.*

"John showed up one day at the auditions for our first national touring company of *Grease*," explains Ken Waissman. "His only experience at that time had been some summer stock work in New Jersey, his home state. But Tom Moore recognized his unique qualities and superior acting talent so we cast him as Doody and

kept him on the road for a year."

Following that, Waissman and Fox brought Travolta to New York, where he played the same role in the Broadway company. Then, they gave him a featured part in their new musical, *Over Here,* which starred the legendary Andrew Sisters.

"Some TV scouts heard his voice on the cast album and came to see him in the show and signed him up."

Lenny Bari plays a principal role in the TV series "Fish;" and the series "Soap" features *Grease* alumnus, Ted Wass.

On the Cloris Leachman show, "Phyllis," you saw Garn Stephens. Even "Mary Hartman, Mary Hartman" had a former "Greaser," Michael Lembeck.

Speaking of soap operas, you're seeing *Grease* players every day. There's Ilene Kristen (Delia Ryan) on "Ryan's Hope;" Meg Bennett (Liz Caslo) on "Search for Tomorrow;" Candice Early (Donna Beck) on "All My Children;" John Driver (Gary Walton) on "Search for Tomorrow."

Former "Greasers" are on view in motion pictures as well. Treat Williams and Jeff Conaway appeared in *The Eagle Has Landed; Between the Lines* featured Marilu Henner; Richard Gere is starring in *Looking for Mr. Goodbar* and is currently shooting *Blood Brothers* at Warners; and Tony Award winner Barry Bostwick will be the star of *Double Feature.*

The four-member Manhattan Transfer singing group, which had its own network TV show features Alan Paul, another member of the *Grease* cast.

The tough casting policies have paid off well. You can be sure that many of the performers you see on stage will soon be familiar faces on TV and movie screens.

Top: The cast in a scene from *Grease.* Bottom: The Pink Ladies and the Burger Palace Boys in a scene from *Grease.*

by Chris Chase

Running with Grease

On the last weekend in May, the New York Post's drama critic, Martin Gottfried, took to task the Dramatists Guild whose members had just voted for their favorite 20th Century American plays and musicals. Decrying the Guild's taste in straight plays ("an esthetic level that is mundane, to put it mildly"), Mr. Gottfried went on to knock their regard for such works as *The Little Foxes* ("prosaic drama"), *Our Town* ("downright embarrassing") and *Awake and Sing* ("outright joke"). Less reprehensible to Mr. Gottfried were Guild members' musical choices. At least, he said, nobody had voted for *Grease*.

Well, drama critics have to live too. I guess. And Lillian Hellman's doing all right, and Clifford Odets doesn't need any defense from me, and that goes double for Thornton Wilder who has probably moved almost as many people as Martin Gottfried.

But what about *Grease?* Though I'd never seen *Grease,* I figured if it was way up there on Mr. G.'s you-know-what list, I was going to be crazy about it, so I decided to take a look.

Easier said than done. *Grease,* it turns out, is a secret weapon of a show; if you could figure out the secret, you'd be rich. *Grease* is a musical, set in the 50's, about the inmates of an institution called Rydell High School, and it has just gone into its fifth year at the Royale Theatre, playing to standees eight times a week.

Ten other things I discovered:

1. Little kids love *Grease*.
2. Old ladies love *Grease*.
3. The doorman at the Royale loves *Grease,* or why did he go rocking down the aisle during the second act, hands waving, head bobbing in time to the music?
4. *Grease* has made it onto the list of the top ten longest-running Broadway shows ever.

5. A national company of *Grease* is going out in October. Again.
6. It will be the third time a national company of *Grease* has gone out. The last national company closed in Philadelphia on New Year's Eve, 1974.
7. *Grease* started the craze for reviving the 50's which craze brought us "American Graffiti," "Happy Days," and a rash of disc jockeys talking about oldies but goodies.
8. Many "Greasers" have gone on to larger fame. Adrienne Barbeau became the daughter of television's "Maude," and John Travolta turned into Vinnie Barbarino on "Welcome Back, Kotter," a fact that causes him to be mobbed by giddy children wherever he appears.
9. Kathi Moss, who plays Cha-Cha, is the only member of the cast who has been with the B'way show from the beginning.
10. In Mexico City, *Grease* was called *Vaselina.* If it's done in France, it will be called *Brilliantine.*

It's 7 P.M. Backstage, some of the actors are already milling about, beginning to make cups of tea and bum cigarettes from one another. A girl sets her hair in electric rollers, and several people discuss the day's baseball game in Central Park. Third baseman Alann Lloyd (when he's not playing third base, he's playing Danny Zuko, the closest thing *Grease* has to a hero) says the *Grease* team was demolished single-handedly by Colleen Dewhurst, playing for the glory of *Who's Afraid of Virginia Woolf?* Any team that has Colleen doesn't need a lot of other players.

In a small upstairs office, Kenneth Waissman and Maxine Fox who (along with Anthony D'Amato) produced *Grease,* are happy to talk about it. Waissman and Fox are married, they grew up in the 50's, they were enthusiastic about the *Grease* music, lyrics and book, by Warren Casey and Jim Jacobs, but they remember being half afraid to do the show. "All the experts told us not to," says Waissman. "They said, '50's music is dead, the clothes were awful, nobody would want to look at any of it again.' We were the war baby generation, the biggest consumer group in the country, but everyone was telling us nobody under 40 would go to B'way."

Well, not only did the war baby generation turn out for *Grease,* so did the teenagers. At this point, so many kids go—in certain high schools, each new junior class ritualistically attends—the older people in the audience are often outnumbered.

Grease is extremely explicit about how painful it is to be an adolescent," says Maxine Fox. "It's a sociological statement. But mostly it's fun."

Watchers tend to agree. Douglass Watt, of the *New York Daily News,* once tried to explain why so many theatregoers were empathizing with the Burger Palace Boys and the Pink Ladies. "Every few minutes or so, after the 'cool' Rydell High class of '59 gets through putting one another on in the cafeteria, burger place and park or at the prom or girls' pajama party," wrote Mr. Watt, "the beat comes on and somebody or other gives his or her all to such heartfelt and almost paralyzing bits of self-expression as 'Beauty School Dropout,' 'It's Raining on Prom Night,' and 'Alone at a Drive-In Movie.' "

Grease tends to be totally raunchy and entirely innocent, a mixing of matrixes so bizarre that it's hard to understand why it works. The Rydell High crowd talks dirty (and they pop bubble gum, and Frenchy dyes her hair hot pink, and the words to "Greased Lightnin,' " an ode to a hot rod, can't even be reprinted here) but they are at heart guileless, uncorrupt.

If you happen to hear a nine-year old who's hooked on the record singing along loudly, you'll know what I'm talking about.

To be sure, not *everybody* is beguiled by *Grease* (I talked to one lady who declared that half those people playing high school kids looked thirty-five years old to her, and anyway, it was a bad idea to glorify teen-aged punks who wore oil-slicked hair) but *most* people are beguiled.

Waissman and Fox say that, for every new *Grease* company they form, they audition between 1500 and 2000 performers "to get the 16 we need." Because everyone in the cast has to act, sing and dance. There's plenty of ensemble work, but no chorus, and each actor gets to do at least one fat bit of his own.

The players seem genuinely to like one another. "The cast is who your friends are," one girl says. "Any time anybody in the cast has a bit in a film, we go to see that film. Same thing if somebody's performing in a showcase or a club. We're all there." (The Broadway cast is presently stocked with people who used to be in other companies of *Grease,* and there are actors all over this city who've played the show, know the roles, and could be rushed into service on ten minutes' notice.)

Lynne Guerra, production stage manager, tells of a kid who left *Grease* two weeks ago—she intends to try her luck in California—but who keeps coming back to the Royale "to iron a shirt, to sew on a button. It's her security blanket."

The set of *Grease* is framed with huge reproductions of pictures of high school kids taken in the 50's. The authors, the producers, their friends all furnished yearbooks for set designer Douglas Schmidt to plunder.

"When we first saw the model, our pictures, mine and Maxine's, weren't there," Kenneth Waissman says. "Then the model went off to the shop, the set was built, and when it was brought into the Royale, we saw the designer had pulled a switch."

There were—and are—Waissman and Fox, large as life, and twice as Greasy looking.

"I remember sitting at the kitchen table at home in Baltimore with the proofs of my pictures," says Waissman. "I kept saying, 'These are disgusting!' until my mother got tired. 'Will you just pick one?' she said. 'You'll never have to look at it again.' "

Waissman shakes his head. "I've been looking at it for four years. I've looked at it on Broadway, in London, in Mexico City—"

If plans work out, he'll be looking at it in Paris, too. Meanwhile, he can laugh all the way to the bank, should anybody happen to ask him if he knows what Martin Gottfried thinks of *Grease.*

'Grease' Is Something Else — —

By DOUGLAS WATT

Rock music, like jazz before it, is uneasy in the legitimate theater. Improvisatory in nature, it can thrive there in its pure form only when the dramatic work it is meant to adorn is informal in itself — as in the case of "Hair" or the exceedingly loose approach to Euripides in the "Iphigenia" evening at the Public Theater. Works such as "Jesus Christ Superstar," "Two Gentlemen of Verona" and "Love Me, Love My Children," though casually referred to as rock musicals, employ the characteristic rock sound to varying degrees but are not essentially rock shows, all three scores being the product of trained composers who incorporate many other forms of music, both popular and classical, in these works.

The excitement of rock, as in jazz, lies in its spontaneity or impression of same. The glory of the musical theater lies in the excitement produced by carefully calculated means, by a combination of intelligence and sensitivity always in control of the effects produced. You could not, for example, imagine the brilliant "Rain in Spain" sequence in "My Fair Lady" being left to chance, even in the hands of the most inspired musicians.

"Grease," which is at the Eden Theater, is something new, a rock musical that is also formal in structure. This is because it is a thoughtful, as well as skillful recreation of a particular period — the mid-50s when rock 'n' roll was bursting upon the consciousness of the young in a spectacular fashion. It was a joyous time in the history of a music that had for decades been confined to the black ghettos, recorded by the major labels only in a category known as "race" and purchased almost exclusively by members of that race. Like jazz, a form distinguished by the addition of the blue note (the minor third) to syncopated music, "race" music, or "rhythm-and-blues" as it came to be known, found its bedrock in the blues and was, of course, basically the black man's music. The white youth of the mid 1950s responded to it en masse only when white musicians (notably Presley, though there were others before him) took it up.

Even so, rock 'n' roll was, aside form an occasional authentic piece such as "Hound Dog," largely a pallid, innocent form of musical expression whose beat was the kicker. It wasn't until the 1960s that the kids were ready for hard rock and increasingly sophisticated variations on the form.

The charm of "Grease" is its ability to capture the innocence and joy of a new pop-culture manifestation. Older people in the midst of it either rejected it entirely or let it slide off their

consciousness while they listened to Vic Damone sing "On the Street Where You Live." "Grease" very modestly but very effectively contains for us that moment in time as if it were imprisoned in one of those glass balls of winter scenes with which you can shake up a snowfall.

Back then, when the rock 'n' roll songs seemed so forgettable, it was funny to imagine a boy and girl of the period 10 or 15 years later, married now and with children of their own, sitting smiling in their living room and saying, as the long-ago sound of "I'm Just a Teenager in Love" emerged from a TV or radio program, "They're playing our song." Well, that's what "Grease" is all about. Every few minutes or so, after the "cool" Rydell High class of '59 gets through putting one another on in the cafeteria, burger place, and park or at the prom or girls' pajama party, the beat comes on and somebody or other gives his or her all to such heartfelt and almost paralyzing bits of self-expression as "Beauty School Dropout," "It's Raining on Prom Night" and "Alone at a Drive-in Movie." The titles alone are impossible to resist.

As I say, "Grease" is very modest in its aims and very sure about them. It succeeds because of the simplicity of its theme and because of the calculated skill with which it is presented. One thing I was surprised to find it do so exhilaratingly was dancing. I suddenly remembered that musicals used to be full of dancing, that often a particular dance number (like the one Ron Field had the good sense to set to the title number in "Applause") could steal the show, that you didn't have to wade through heavy dramatic scenes only to find heavily "integrated" songs at the end of them.

The procedure in "Grease" is some lines of brisk chatter by the boys in ducktailed hairdos and the girls in fluffy ones and whoosh! they're into a dance. And the dances are excellent ones by a young choreographer named Patricia Birch who could probably revitalize Broadway all by herself. Everything about the evening — Tom Moore's direction, Douglas W. Schmidt's basic scenic effect created by photo blow-ups, the loud but carefully-engineered instrumental support and, best of all, the performance by a bright cast — is "keen," as we would have said in my own high school days.

"Grease" is a tonic.

JOHN TRAVOLTA

DANNY

John Travolta is success electrified. The exciting young man w
thrilled millions of theatre goers in "Saturday Night Fever" h
again made his way to stardom in the sensational Paramou
release GREASE.

Now 24, John grew up in Englewood, New Jersey where
was surrounded by a family atmosphere of show business. He
the youngest of the six Travolta children, all of whom are thea
rically inclined. Ellen, 37, is the oldest, and acts in pilots for C
and NBC. Margaret, 32, is doing TV and voice-overs in Chicag
Anne, 29, is acting in New York City. Sam Jr., 34, performed
"Dial M for Murder" while serving in the military in Europe, a
now is organizing his own band. Joey, 27, is also looking for t
bright lights and has been promised a screen test.

No doubt one of the biggest influences on John's early acting developement was his mother. Helen Travolta is a veteran of show business — one of the Sunshine Sisters on Hackensack radio in the 1930's — and has filled the past two decades as an actress, director, and drama coach.

From the age of four, John has held fast to wanting to become an actor. He knew he would be a star even when he danced in his living room with James Cagney doing dance steps during a TV rerun of Yankee Doodle Dandy. At the age of nine, John was in his first performance, an Actor's Studio production of "Who'll Save the Plowboy."

All during his younger years, John felt the magnetism of nearby Broadway and at the age of 16 he dropped out of school and left home to try his luck in professional show business. "I decided I was good enough to compete with the professionals," he recalls. "So I went into New York City."

During his first year in the Big Apple, John stayed with his sister Anne, and in no time started his sure rise to fame by landing roles in "Gypsy" and "Bye Bye Birdie." Later, at the age of 18, John was on the road with the acclaimed Broadway "Grease" company, in which he played Doody.

Eager for success and more demanding roles than he found on the stage, John headed West. But his beginning in films was slow. He made his first Hollywood movie appearance in a horror show called "The Devil's Rain." John felt positive about the movie and his performance — despite that towards the end of the film he melts into a small puddle while shouting, "Blasphemer! Blasphemer!" From scenes of puddles and lines of "Blasphemer!" John pole-vaulted into the highly regarded TV series "Welcome Back Kotter." As Barbarino, John made himself a star and a teen idol to millions of admirers. Long before the series began its thunderous run, John recognized the stellar impact the part of Barbarino would have on his acting career and his audiences. Admirers started calling him the "new TV

hood, the Kotter show's answer to the Fonz." And as might b expected, four-color posters were appearing all over.

By this time John had become a home-screen favorite and wa chosen for the dramatic TV movie "The Boy in the Plastic Bub ble." He played opposite the beautiful and sensitive Diana Hy land. John and Diana spent much of their professional and pr vate time together while they were making "Bubble," and romance blossomed. Even though Diana was 18 years John senior, neither one felt there was a problem with the differenc in their ages.

The real life love story had no happy ending. Diana's story

very much unlike John's. John was in Brooklyn filming "Saturday Night Fever" when he received word from the West coast that Diana had taken a turn for the worse from a shocking battle with cancer. The man who was building a world dropped everything and quickly flew back to California.

John's career skyrocketed with his performance in "Saturday Night Fever." He received extraordinary critical acclaim and won the Best Actor Award from the National Board of Review as well as recognition by the New York Film Critics Circle, and The National Society of Film Critics. Topping all awards was John's nomination as Best Actor in the 1977 Academy Awards.

Time Magazine described his performance as "a revelation." Newsweek called it "a triumphant starring debut" and his dancing "spectacular." Pauline Kael in The New Yorker wrote "Travolta is such an original presence. He goes so far inside the role he seems incapable of a false note . . . He acts like someone who loves to dance and more than that, he acts like someone who loves to act." Vincent Canby wrote "John Travolta displays the kind of galvanizing energy that commands serious attention," and David Sheehan hailed his as "the most exciting new screen presence to come along since the early days of Brando, Dean, and Newman."

The smash hit movie "Saturday Night Fever" grew out of the 1976 New York Magazine story "Tribal Rites of the New Saturday Night," by Nik Cohn, a British writer. Cohn did extensive research in Brooklyn searching for the "new generation" of the 1970's, the clusters of young people who seemed oblivious to the progress-centered world surrounding them. Cohn discovered the perfect group he had been searching for in Bay Ridge and called them "the Faces." This "new generation" are the everywhere people who work at their monotonous jobs all week, and then for one brief night — Saturday night — they change, they become somebody important, if only in their unknown little groups.

From "Saturday Night Fever" John has stepped into the limelight once again with his performance in GREASE.

Five years ago Pat Birch, GREASE'S choreographer, cast John as Doody in the national company of "Grease." Ms. Birch remarked to Tom Buckley of the New York Times in a recent interview, "When I saw him audition, I said to myself, 'There's something there.' He's a wonderfully imaginative performer and tremendously cooperative when you've earned his trust. Most of the funny business in the baseball scene in 'Grease,' for example, was his own invention. I'm very fond of him. One day when we were filming the auto-race scene in 'Grease' at the Los Angeles River, I asked him, 'What do you want to do when you grow up?' He said, 'Well, Paul Newman's had a pretty good career.' "

OLIVIA NEWTON-JOHN

Olivia Newton-John, the internationally popular, award-winning recording artist, makes her starring film debut in GREASE. Olivia is one of the most honored female vocalists ever, with accolades including three Grammy Awards, a total of eight American Music Awards, and numerous other recognitions. Her recordings of ''Let Me Be There,'' ''If You Love Me, Let Me Know,'' ''Have You Never Been Mellow,'' and ''Please Mister Please'' have all been Certified Gold million-sellers, and her smash ''I Honestly Love You'' has been Certified Platinum. In addition, all of her albums have been Gold, and four of them have also gone on to Platinum distinction.

SANDY

Born in Cambridge, England, Olivia spent most of her life in Melbourne, Australia. At the age of 16 she found her way back to Great Britain by way of a talent contest which soon landed her a recording career. In 1973, she was awarded her first Grammy as Best Female Country Vocalist for "Let Me Be There." The very next year "I Honestly Love You" won her a pair of Grammys for Record of the Year and Best Pop Vocal Performance.

Olivia was named top female vocalist in 1975 by both Billboard and Cashbox. She received the People's Choice Award for Favorite Musical Performer in both 1974 and 1976 and has been named favorite female vocalist at the American Music Awards every year since 1974.

When talking about her starring role in GREASE, Olivia says, "It's really been a complete change for me — a complete breakthrough from what I've been doing. It's always nice to try something different, and to extend oneself a little bit — which is what I hope I've been doing."

Performing in GREASE with John Travolta and Stockard Channing, Olivia was signed on by producers Allan Carr and Robert Stigwood when the company was already into pre-filming rehearsals.

"I had met Olivia at a small dinner party given by Helen Reddy and Jeff Wald about four months earlier," Carr recalls. "I'd never seen her in person before, and I couldn't resist telling her that she really should be doing movies. I mean, she's just adorable and yet she has a very special sophistication about her, too. I knew if we could just capture that on film, we would have our Sandy."

Even though Olivia was about to leave on a cross-country tour at the time, winding up at the Metropolitan Opera House in New York, and from there a six-week tour of Europe, she agreed to the screen test with John Travolta. Fortunately, that screen-test went perfectly, and Olivia reported the very next day for rehearsals.

"Actually, I had done one film before, about six years ago," Olivia admits. "But I'm really trying to forget it. It opened and closed in about a week in England, and never played in America, so I'm really counting GREASE as my first."

Olivia's flair for musical comedy led to a pair of highly prized television specials for the BBC and ABC. And, on her last tour of Europe, she made a special guest appearance on the Silver Jubilee television show honoring Queen Elizabeth II in the 25th year of her reign. And then followed GREASE.

"When I first saw the show in London about 5 years ago, I never thought I would ever be playing Sandy," Olivia recalls. "I loved the show, but actually I think the fact that the role has been changed so that the girl has moved from Australia to the United States has helped make Sandy more interesting. It explains why she is so different from everyone else, and it makes her innocence more believeable. I remember when I first came here, and although I wasn't as naive as Sandy by then — I had already had a career in Europe — I can identify with why she finds it all so strange."

Asked about the emphasis on dancing in her first major film, Olivia remembers with a laugh: "People on the set used to kid John and me — saying 'Watch out, Fred and Ginger.' Filming the hop was probably the most fun, and I'd love to dance again in films — if they let me."

T-BIRDS

SONNY

PUTZIE   DOODY

KENICKIE

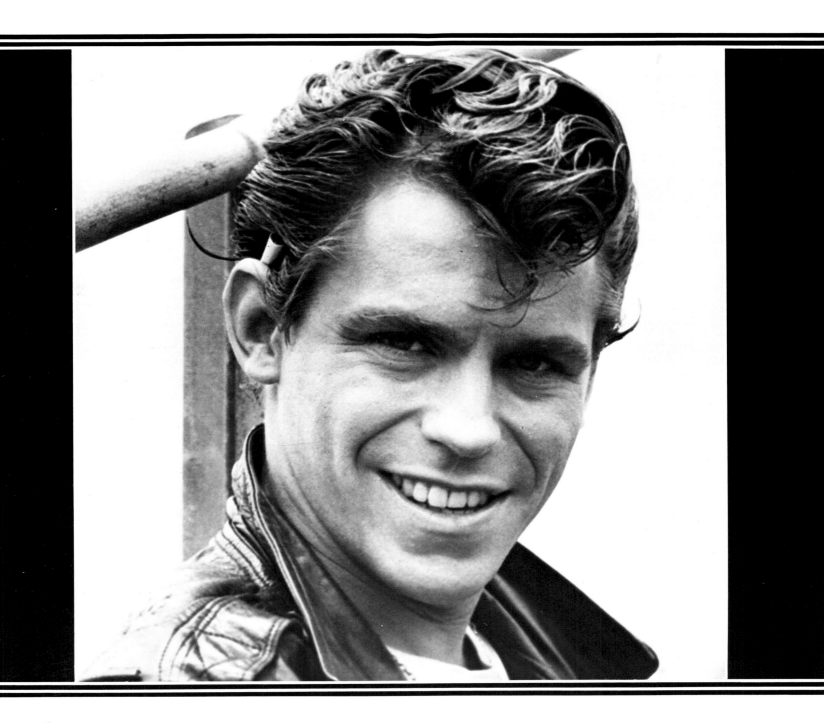

Jeff Conaway

Actor Jeff Conaway plays the role of Kenickie in GREASE.

At the age of ten Jeff found himself on Broadway in "All the Way Home," directed by Arthur Penn. "It was great. When I finished auditioning I was walking away and I heard a voice saying, 'Hey, you . . . stay.' Well, I started looking around — I figured he couldn't be talking to me. And then Arthur Penn came running up onto the stage, asking me what I had done before. And I told him that I had played Eliza Doolittle's father in the first grade, and he laughed. But then I got a call — it was on my tenth birthday, right in the middle of my party — and the play ran for a year on Broadway."

Following his early success Conaway appeared with the national company of "Critics' Choice," a series of television commercials, and a year with a rock and roll group touring with such Sixties groups as the Animals, Herman's Hermits and Chuck Berry.

Years later — after attending the North Carolina School of the Arts and NYU, doing a couple of "Yellow Pages" commercials, playing Billy the Kid in 'Wanted' at Judson Poet's Theatre and taking a role in the movie "Jenifer on My Mind" — yes, years later came GREASE for Jeff Conaway.

It was GREASE. ''I came into the run about two weeks after the show opened, and then I replaced Barry Bostwick as Danny,'' Jeff explains. ''I never thought I'd be playing Kenickie in the film, but the difference between my Kenickie and the one on stage is that I play the role smarter. My Kenickie knows what he wants to say, but he can't get it out unless he's being a wisecracker. That's why I'm always smoking, or eating. On stage, Kenickie would have a lead pipe in his hand and there would be no doubt in your mind that he would use it. With me, the lead pipe may look right, but somehow you know that it's all image. There's a sensitivity underneath.''

Some time later after Jeff left the Broadway show of GREASE he thundered onto the screen by appearing in the all-star ''The Eagle Has Landed,'' Disney's loving and warm Christmas release, ''Pete's Dragon,'' and the critically-acclaimed ''I Never Promised You a Rose Garden.''

The change from stage to screen for Jeff has been a maturing process filled with gains and losses. ''On stage you're in front of flats; for film you're in a real high school and you don't have to work at that,'' Jeff remarks. ''As long as you stay open and know what you want to do, and you know what you want to achieve in a scene, you just let it flow. You go with it. And if it's wrong, you do it over again. I miss the live audience of theatre, but making movies is much more fun.''

DOODY

Barry Pearl, who plays Doody, has been in show business ever since he was . . . you guessed it . . . a baby. Now 28, he claims that the doctor in the delivery room was his first audience.

Barry debuted on Broadway at the age of 11 in ''Bye, Bye, Birdie,'' and has had an active career with featured roles in the Broadway and touring companies of ''Oliver!'' and the national companies of ''You're A Good Man, Charlie Brown,'' and GREASE, both staged by GREASE choreographer Pat Birch.

''I had done the role of Sonny in the national tour,'' explains Barry Pearl. ''John Travolta was Doody in that company, so you can see how much the role has changed. I'm playing Doody as the comic of the group. I tried to incorporate what I learned back in the 50's about comedy into the role. Doody is the proverbial class clown. Jerry Lewis is Doody's idol, and I think he will become a professional stand-up comic,'' Barry predicts. ''I was weaned on the Three Stooges and, in a more sophisticated way, on the Marx Brothers. So playing Doody this way has come very natural to me. But Doody's a mixture. He's not one-sided. The character of Doody is very much like Sonny. It's really my characterization of Sonny.''

SONNY

Michael Tucci plays a more serious and mature Sonny in the film. Oddly enough, Michael was a fully accredited lawyer before he gave up the court room for the calling of the silver screen. "I always wanted to do it — my undergraduate work was in theatre — but I never had the nerve to just go out and audition," Michael admits. "I was a lawyer in New York for 11 weeks when a friend of mine arranged for me to go up for 'Fiddler on the Roof.' I went in — I even had my three-piece suit on — and sang a song and I got the role of Motel, the tailor." Next for Michael Tucci came the national companies of "Godspell" and "Grease."

"A young Marty. That's what Sonny is," Claims Tucci. "He's like the mediator of the group. He's middle of the road. And I think Sonny has some smarts too. He'll get it together in a couple of years. But most of all he's sensitive."

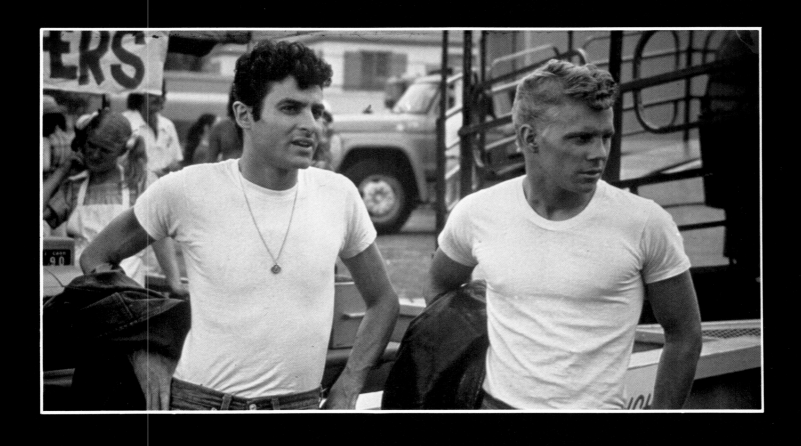

PUTZIE

Putzie, the youngest of the T-Birds, is played by actor Kelly Ward. Kelly is the only member of the group whose family background is theatre. "My whole family was into show business," he reflects. "My mom and dad were a dance team. Now they're choreo/directors for the San Diego Civic Light Opera. I guess I always knew that I would follow them into the business, and I took ballet and modern jazz as a kid."

Kelly went to New York when he was 18. "It was sort of a scary place at first; I didn't know anybody," he explains. He was quickly discovered by Pat Birch, GREASE's choreographer who cast him in her contemporary Broadway rock-musical, "Truck Load." Later Kelly starred in the Academy Award-winning student film, "The Preparatory," which led to an appearance in director Randal Kleiser's "The Boy in the Plastic Bubble," starring John Travolta.

"I think Putzie is basically down to earth like the other guys," explains Ward about his character. "But he's more subdued. He's the youngest, and I think he's been more sheltered than the others. He needs something to hang on to. He has different reasons for being in the gang; maybe he's missing a father and he needs older brothers. But he's a little more shy, a little less inclined to do crazy things. He gets more involved when he gets excited."

PINK LADIES

RIZZO

MARTY   FRENCHY

JAN

"It's barbecue smoke instead of back alleys."

Stockard first received popular attention for her praised performance on Broadway in the Tony Award-winning musical, "Two Gentlemen of Verona." Then she appeared in Mike Nichol's "The Fortune." Very few movie-goers will forget Stockard as the zany heiress Jack Nicholson and Warren Beatty plotted to sabotage.

After "The Fortune," Stockard found herself in "The Big Bus" and then loving "Sweet Revenge." She later co-starred opposite Peter Falk in the Neil Simon comedy, "The Cheap Detective," which kept Stockard running from set to set and changing several costumes because filming Simon's play overlapped into the shooting schedule of GREASE.

Stockard Channing was born in New York and attended school at Radcliffe. Unkowingly even to herself then, she was preparing for her absorbing performance in GREASE in her childhood years of the Fifties. "I was a little sister in that period," she says. "But my sister was in high school and between the two of us I do remember very distinctly the mores of the time."

"GREASE isn't like any other film I've done before," the veteran actress explains. "It's a musical, and it's very light. Your character emerges out of this moment-to-moment behavior with the people around you. You can't try to set it up."

"This is the fifth film I've done, and it's funny how they've all been different. In a production of this size, the only problem is that as an actor I miss the intimacy of working one-on-one with the director. Largely, in this picture, I think what has happened is that the actors have worked with each other — and from that something emerges. And if director Randal (Kleiser) doesn't like something, he will work with us to adjust it. That's very different from working with a Mike Nichols who must be on top of every detail. But Randal's style certainly seems to be working out best for this particular film."

One of the most entertaining parts of the movie for film audiences is the pair of musical numbers Stockard has created for the film. "I do 'Look at Me, I'm Sandra Dee,'" Rizzo says, "as a total comedy number — girls at a slumber party. It's very funny, and they've changed the placement of the song so that it works better for comedy.

"But the other song, 'There are Worse Things I Could Do' — I do love that song. In the first script they had cut it, and I can understand why. It's a heavy, dramatic number. In the play Rizzo sings the song to Sandy, but in the film it's essentially about herself, to herself. It's more like a monologue, and more about her relationship with Kinickie, her boyfriend."

When Stockard compares the film & play versions she recognizes the thin lines that separate the two. "But you also have to remember that the film we're doing is very different from the play. There's no villain in this piece, and I think on stage there was much more of one. Rizzo was darker, perhaps, than I am. This is very sunny. It's barbecue smoke instead of back alleys."

MARTY

Dinah Manoff is GREASE'S loveable Marty and daughter of Academy Award-winning actress Lee Grant. Dinah is the youngest of the vibrant Pink Ladies.

She's been seen on TV in the all-star "Raid on Entebbe," in "Welcome Back Kotter," and in the "Great Cherub."

Oddly enough, when the full cast for GREASE was ready to sail Dinah had almost elected not to jump aboard. "I was up for another part at the time, and I was really into getting that one. After the first audition I told my agent to forget GREASE, and then I got my callback. That's when I really started to get excited about the film."

Playing Marty has been Dinah's first big chance to play a role which has enabled her to blossom. "Marty is just starting to learn how to use her sexuality to get what she wants," Dinah says. "Now granted, it comes off looking very silly when at 16 you think you can manipulate people by using your sexuality. I play the sex pot. I play Marty as working extra hard to throw her weight around — her toughness is an act, a cover up. By the end she develops a sensitivity for a guy her own age. Until that time, I think she's been dating her older sister's friends."

"I attribute the fact that it works so well to the fantasy of GREASE. They don't ask you to believe it. It's fantasy. It's pure entertainment.

And GREASE will open doors to more musicals," Dinah predicts. "It has definitely started a trend."

"At the end, I felt like I was graduating from high school."

"Look at me, I'm Sandra Dee."

JAN

Jamie Donnelly plays the dieting, late bloomer, Jan in GREASE, and this performance marks her first step onto the silver screen. Jamie was born in John Travolta's hometown in Englewood, New Jersey. Before coming to GREASE she was a hit in the off-Broadway performance of "You're a Good Man, Charlie Brown." Then she launched onto Broadway with "George M," "Grease," "Rogers and Hart Tonight," and the sizzling "The Rocky Horror Show."

Although Jamie played the role of Jan in the Broadway version, she found the screen role character sharply more complex — yet intensely more interesting. "I had done the role on Broadway some time ago, and the time spent there seemed to be enough for one part. But the character had developed considerably in the transition from stage to film, and that made it much more interesting to me," Jamie explains.

"Jan on stage made no transition at all," Jamie remarks as she again considers her role as Jan. "She was just sort of this fat sloppy kid. In the film she's a late bloomer. She falls in love and she becomes aware of herself as a physical person. It isn't just that she diets. She becomes persentable for whatever might follow."

Jamie speaks well for the camaraderie for not only the Pink Ladies but for the entire cast: "Being together for 12 hours each day, we became a gang. We came to really feel that way about each other. At the end, I felt like I was graduating from high school — it was that kind of a real and total experience. And that's fulfilling."

Frenchy's friendship with Sandy is one of the most memorable parts of GREASE.

FRENCHY

Didi Conn is the always fun-loving helpful, and caring Frenchy in GREASE. She came to GREASE with a long list of notable roles. She starred in "You Light Up My Life" for Columbia Pictures, and in "High School" for Universal. Her voice is remembered as the voice of Raggedy Ann in Twentieth Century-Fox's animated film version of "Raggedy Ann and Andy." But that's not the sum of Didi's success before her appearance in GREASE. She appeared as a guest star on TV's highly successful "Happy Days." She then teamed up with Danny Thomas and played his pixieish receptionist on the NBC comedy series, "The Practice." Didi then found herself in a starring role with Henry Winkler in "Room Service," a production of the Marx Brothers comedy classic.

"Frenchy has a premature, very strong career goal," Didi comments. Her only ambition up until this point is to go to beauty school. She cares about people and she wants to make everyone beautiful. But she finds out that beauty school isn't what she thought it would be, and she also learns that she has a lot of friends who care about her. She's come back to school for a fresh start. And to start enjoying herself as a teenager," Didi explains as she shows her closeness and talented understanding of the character Frenchy.

SPECIAL GUESTS

SHA-NA-NA

JOHNNY CASINO
AND
THE GAMBLERS

EVE ARDEN
PRINCIPAL MCGEE

EVE ARDEN

Eve Arden won love and admiration from all Americans as the all-time favorite English teacher, ''Our Miss Brooks.'' She also won an acclaimed Emmy for that cherished role. In GREASE, Ms. Arden takes on the new role of Principal McGee of the fictional Rydell High.

In her earlier acting years Ms. Arden headed east from her hometown of Mill Valley, California, carrying along hope, young talent and a suitcase, to star on Broadway in ''Ziegfeld Follies of 1936'' and ''. . . 1938.'' Later she returned to sunny California and to starring roles in such films as ''Stage Door,'' in which she held her own in an all-star cast headed by Katherine Hep-

burn and Ginger Rogers, ''Cover Girl,'' ''Night and Day,'' and ''Mildred Pierce,'' for which she received an Academy Award nomination.

For GREASE, Ms. Arden has been promoted from English Teacher to principal — a well-deserved promotion. She welcomes back to the fall school term both students and faculty. She finds Sonny (Michael Tucci) lingering in the halls and awards him after school eraser dusting duty. Ms. Arden is on hand to greet Coach Calhoun (Sid Caesar), Automotive Shop teacher Mrs. Murdock (Alice Ghostly), and the dithering and sentimental school secretary (Dody Goodman).

TEEN ANGEL
FRANKIE AVALON

Frankie Avalon is GREASE's Teen Angel. The Fifties teen idol and national heartthrob sings and dances in a special fantasy musical sequence that electrifies audiences while it leaves the troubled Frenchy love-struck.

In the actual Fifties, Frankie Avalon's recording of "Venus" was one of the biggest million seller hits of the decade. In 1959 he was named "King of Song" by the Disc Jockey's Association and received Photoplay Magazine's Gold Award for Most Popular Vocalist.

Mr. Avalon is well remembered for his 'beach party' movies. He starred opposite Annette Funicello in such films as "Beach Party," "Beach Blanket Bingo," and "Bikini Beach." He also starred with John Wayne in "The Alamo" and in "Voyage to the Bottom of the Sea." Avalon has been an ever-popular attraction in Las Vegas and has taken his nightclub act to supper clubs across the country. He is also continually sought out to serve as hosts for teenage beauty pageants.

What audiences across the nation didn't see in GREASE was an off-screen reunion between Avalon and other notable stars. After Avalon finished turning out the Beauty School Dropout fantasy number, he was reteamed with Annette Funicello for a Dick Clark reunion. The Fifties came alive once again.

JOAN BLONDELL

VI

JOAN BLONDELL

True to form, Joan Blondell guest stars in GREASE as Vi, the fast-talking and sympathetic waitress down at the local malt shop who is everyone's confidante with a heart of gold. Joan began in show business at the age of three by upstaging her vaudevillian parents. The blonde veteran of films, theatre, and television played on Broadway in "Ziegfeld Follies" and "Penny Arcade." In 1930 she appeared in "Sinner's Holiday" for which she received an enthusiastic reception from theatre goers. She went on to appear in "Gold Diggers of 1933," and ". . . 1937," "Stage Struck," "Footlight Parade," "Three Men on a Horse" and "A Tree Grows in Brooklyn." She began the Fifties with an Academy Award nomination for "The Blue Veil." She went on to star opposite Tracy and Hepburn in "Desk Set," and with June Allyson, Ann Miller, and Ann Sheridan in the all-star cast of leading ladies in "The Opposite Sex." Joan returned to the stage in 1971 and received applause for her role in "The Effects of Gamma Rays on Man-In-The Moon Marigolds." More recently she starred in the film "The Cincinnati Kid," featuring Steve McQueen. Joan just recently completed John Cassavetes film, "Opening Night."

DODY GOODMAN

As expected, Dody Goodman turns up even more confused and zany than ever in GREASE as 'Principal' Eve Arden's secretary. Dody first achieved stardom as a resident crazy on Jack Paar's original "Tonight" show. She has just completed her role as the always-perplexed mother of "Mary Hartman, Mary Hartman." A television celebrity whose appearances on "The Merv Griffin Show," "Dinah" and "The Liar's Club" are always a delight, Ms. Goodman recently starred in Norman Lear's "Mary Hartman" spin-off, "Fernwood 2 Night." Dody was also seen last year in Mel Brook's "Silent Movie."

In GREASE when Dody's not banging away on the xylophone for Eve Arden she's cheering Rydell High's athletic team on to victory or bouncing around the dance floor.

DODY GOODMAN

BLANCHE

EDD BYRNES
VINCE FONTAINE

EDD BYRNES

As the star of television's favorite "77 Sunset Strip," Edd Byrnes became "Kookie" to America in the Fifties. His famous recording of "Kookie, Kookie, Lend Me Your Comb" even netted him a Gold record. Since then, Edd has had his own television show in Europe, has starred in such films as "Fear Strikes Out" and "Girl on the Run," and has toured in productions of "The Owl and the Pussycat," "Picnic," and "Bus Stop."

One of the first teen idols of all time, Edd remembers when he would just comb his hair and the girls would squeal. "This is where I came in," mused Edd when he saw today's teens run-

ning for Travolta's autograph. Appropriately enough, Byrnes plays Vince Fontaine in the film, GREASE's National Bandstand host-with-the-most.

Asked about his performance in the musical, Edd replies, "I was amused by the whole thing. I didn't pattern my character after anyone. I just kept thinking that I'd like to make love to every girl there. And I was just trying to have a good time."

"Making GREASE," Edd adds, "Was fun. Lots of fun. The movie has a lot for everybody — adults and children."

SID CAESAR

COACH CALHOUN

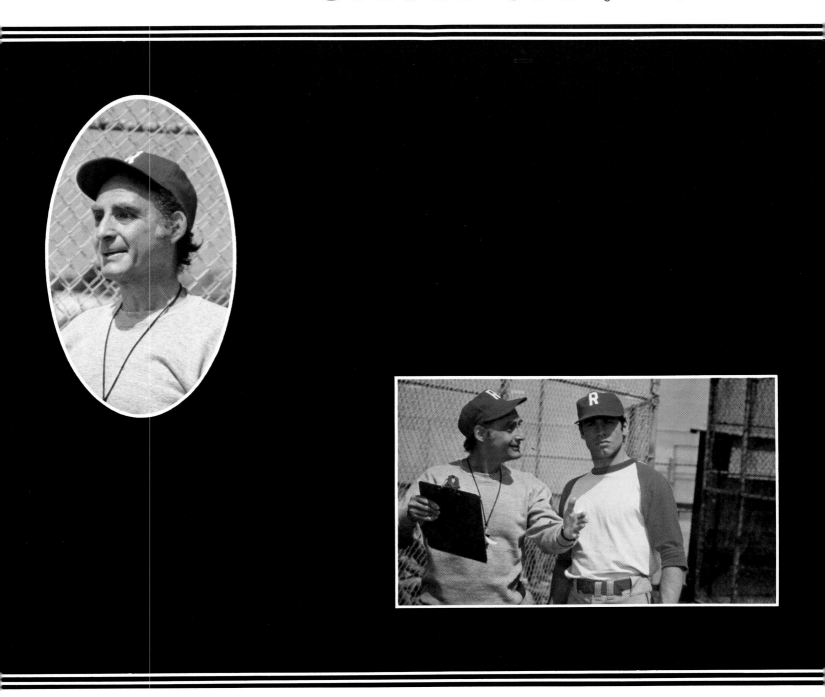

SID CAESAR

Sid Caesar takes to the field as the all around Rydell High Coach Calhoun in GREASE. Sid has been one of the kings of comedy ever since the very early days of television. He was first loved for his part in "The Admiral Broadway Revue." His "Your Show of Shows" series remains a classic, and TV audiences have been fortunate to see the Emmy winning comedian on series and specials ever since. Sid can always be remembered for his starring role in the wild and zany farce "It's a Mad, Mad, Mad, Mad World." From Yonkers, New York, Sid has starred recently in Mel Brooks' "Silent Movie," and has just finished shooting Neil Simon's "The Cheap Detective" for Ray Stark.

In GREASE, Sid leads Danny through a hilarious series of basketball, wrestling, baseball, and track trials that all seem to turn out well in the end of the movie when Danny shows up at the graduation carnival wearing a letter sweater. Still the veteran actor he is, Sid faced another first for his acting career in the movie. In the final shot as Coach Calhoun, Sid gets a pie in the face. Actually, it took five pies before Caesar finally got the rounder square in the face. But all the while, the loveable comedian came up with one-liners to make the extended pie-throwing scene work.

ALICE GHOSTLEY
MRS. MURDOCK

ALICE GHOSTLEY

With screw drivers and wrenches dangling from the pockets of her overalls, Alice Ghostley appears as none other than Mrs. Murdock, the Automotive Shop Teacher. Born in Eve, Missouri, Alice was a long-time comic highlight of television's popular "Bewitched" series. Alice was discovered on Broadway in "New Faces of '52," along with an impressive list of then-newcomers including Paul Lynde, Eartha Kitt, and Carol Lawrence. She went on to star off-Broadway in "The House of Blue Leaves" and on Broadway in "The Sign in Sidney Brustein's Window," for which she won the Tony Award, The New York Drama Critics Circle Award, and Saturday Review's Award. Film audiences have seen her in "To Kill a Mockingbird," "The Graduate," Burt Reynolds' "Gator" and teamed up with Joan Rivers in "Rabbit Test."

SCORPIONS

THE RACE

T-BIRDS

SCORPIONS

DIRECTOR

Film director Randal Kleiser hits one of his many film career goals with the directing of GREASE. At thirty, Kleiser is one of the youngest directors working in Hollywood.

Born in Philadelphia, Kleiser had moved to Los Angeles at the age of 18 to attend University of Southern California's prestigious film school. During his academic training he directed the award winning, one minute "Foot Fetish," about a pair of sneakers making love, and "Peege," his moving, 28-minute Master's project which won top awards at the Atlanta, Cine, Educational, and U.S.A. Film Festivals.

After Kleiser completed his masters he went in search of a directing career. He showed "Peege" to Universal and was offered a non-exclusive contract in their television division.

Other than his formal training, Kleiser recalls another important aspect of his life which enabled him to direct GREASE with much more insight. Randal Kleiser started as an extra in several movies during his early years. "It was when I was at film school, from around 18 to 20 years old. I did a lot of the Elvis movies, and some of the AIP beach movies with Frankie Avalon. And I was in 'Camelot.' So I was around musicals, and I saw a lot of them made. It gave me the opportunity to see how directors cover a musical number.

Starting in TV with "Marcus Welby, M.D.," Kleiser went on to direct other series, most notably the highly acclaimed "Family" for which he directed the pilot episode. Producer Robert Stigwood gave Kleiser his initial opportunity to direct a made-for-TV film, the sensitive "All Together Now." Kleiser's "Dawn: Portrait of a Teenage Runaway" was enthusiastically received by critics and public alike, and his "The Boy in the Plastic Bubble" introduced TV audiences to a different John Travolta.

Kleiser finds directing movies right down his alley. "In television, or in the television movies I've made, there are six pages to do a day, where in episodic TV there are ten pages a day," he comments. I have to do everything — there's just no time to ask anybody," Kleiser says of TV. "On GREASE we have two or three pages a day; there's time to talk, and to think, and to work things out."

I also like the vastness. 'The Ten Commandments' is the movie that made me want to become a director. The parting of the Red Sea, I'd say. I saw that and wanted to direct. It's all I could imagine doing."

Just before the filming of GREASE, Kleiser completed filming "The Gathering," starring Maureen Stapleton and Edward Asner. But Randal found no difficulty — in changing from the seasoned professional to the many young newcomers in GREASE.

"Since I'm close to their age, they treat me more like one of them," he says. "They'll say, 'How about this, 'and they'll work out routines. Then I can mold what they've come up with. It's more like a group effort.

"They don't have any qualms about coming up with new ways, alternate ways; they haven't been taught that the director is sacred. And I don't see how a film like GREASE could have come together in any other way."

PRODUCERS

DAVE FRIEDMAN PHOTO

With top stars as clients and headline and money making movies as properties, ALLAN CARR is one of Hollywood's most celebrated personal managers and producers. A leading denizen of the "new" Hollywood, Carr has been profiled in both TIME and PEOPLE magazines and is the executive consultant for this year's 50th Anniversary presentation of the Academy Awards.

Over the past several years he has represented and guided the careers of some of the most exciting personalities in the entertainment field. A partial list of Carr's clients has included Ann-Margret, Peter Sellers, Nancy Walker, triple-Oscar-winner Marvin Hamlisch, Stockard Channing, Melina Mercouri, Frankie Valli and the Four Seasons, Marisa Berenson, Tony Curtis, Herb Alpert and the Tijuana Brass, Dyan Cannon, Paul Anka, Petula Clark, Sonny Bono and the late Cass Elliot.

Carr served as creative consultant to The Robert Stigwood Organization in the marketing and promotion of "Tommy," the movie rock opera which racked up theatre rentals in excess of $40 million throughout the world. He and Stigwood then presented "Survive!," the cinematic saga of the Andes crash victims which became one of the top grossing international film successes of 1976. Carr previously produced "The First Time," starring Jacqueline Bisset, for United Artists, and "C.C. and Company," with Ann-Margret and Joe Namath, for Avco Embassy.

After finding success in the producing of plays and television shows, Carr became the assistant to Nicholas Ray on Samuel Bronston's "King of Kings," which filmed on location in Madrid for MGM. Soon thereafter, Carr migrated to California where he took an unknown University of Southern California student and presented her in the West Coast premiere of Norman Krasna's comedy, "Sunday in New York." The student was Marlo Thomas and the show, which flourished in Los Angeles for a nine-month engagement, launched the young actress as a major talent. It also did much to establish Carr as a major talent scout.

Currently living in Beverly Hills, Carr also enjoys a well-deserved reputation for giving the most imaginative and glorious of Hollywood parties. His soirees for such luminaries as Elton John, Rudolf Nureyev and Neil Sedaka have become legendary — although none can compare to his black tie dinner dance given in honor of Truman Capote in the Los Angeles Lincoln Heights jail.

In the past few years, ROBERT STIGWOOD has become one of the most influential figures in show business and heads a group of companies that encompasses theatre, films, television, recordings, personal management, concert tours and music publishing.

Born in Adelaide, Australia in 1934 and educated at Sacred Heart College, Robert Stigwood began his career as a copywriter for a local advertising agency and then, at 21, left his home on a ship bound for England. A series of first jobs led to his opening a London theatrical agency. He began casting commercials for television and soon was producing records for many of his clients. In time, he became the first independent record producer in Great Britain.

During the middle 1960's, Stigwood joined forces for a while with Brian Epstein, the manager of the Beatles, to become co-manager of NEMS Enterprises. After Epstein's death, Stigwood

went on to form his own company and launched the careers of, among others, the Bee Gees and Cream.

Moving into the world of theatre in 1968, Robert chose for his first venture the American rock musical, "Hair," a great success which ran for more than five years on London's West End. He followed with highly successful productions of "Jesus Christ Superstar," "Pippin" and "Oh! Calcutta!"

Robert then entered into film production and produced the motion picture version of "Jesus Christ Superstar" in association with the film's director, Norman Jewison. The Stigwood film production of "Tommy," directed by Ken Russell and starring Ann-Margret and Roger Daltrey was one of 1975's most popular films and marked the first truly successful merger of rock music and film to tell a story.

RSO Records, which Stigwood founded in 1973, records the music of the Bee Gees, Eric Clapton, Yvonne Eilliman, Paul

When GREASE has its film premieres around the world in 1978, it will have a variety of appropriate titles for each territory. According to producer Allan Carr, it will be known as "Brilliantino" in Italy, as "Gummina" in France, and GREASE will be dubbed "Vaselina" in Mexico.

To re-create the Fifties for film, the GREASE crew had to supply the actors with some unusual props. For example, the cast chewed about 100,000 pieces of bubble gum over the course of the summer — all on screen. As much as 5,000 pieces disappeared on some days, but, of course, that might be because the actors and extras dispensed with the jaw-tiring prop as soon as the director called "cut."

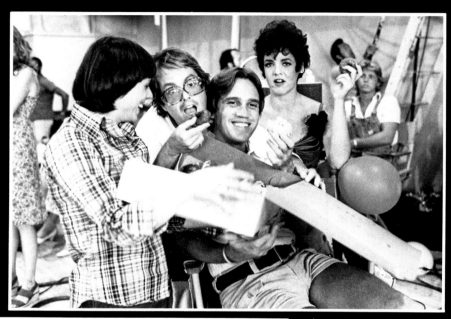

DAVE FRIEDMAN PHOTO

Nicholas, Player and Andy Gibb, as well as the many other new artists Robert continually adds to the successful label. In addition, the RSO label releases all motion picture soundtrack albums of Stigwood productions.

Stigwood's most recent dazzler with John Travolta, "Saturday Night Fever," has proved to be one of the biggest all-time money makers in movie history. He produced "Grease" in association with Allan Carr, and has yet another spectacular movie musical in "Sgt. Pepper's Lonely Hearts Club Band."

To make "GREASE" shine, Stigwood and Carr assembled a cast and crew to rival that of all other musical productions in film history. One couple Carr eyed for the leads early on was Elvis Presley and Ann-Margret. Later he considered Henry Winkler and Susan Dey, until the Fonz decided not to do any more 50's material. But John Travolta, America's #1 heartthrob as Vinnie Barbarino on the top-rated "Welcome Back Kotter" series, was

everyone's first choice to play the role of Danny Zuko on the screen. Fresh from filming "Saturday Night Fever" (for which he received extraordinary acclaim and awards, including an Academy Award nomination as Best Actor) for Stigwood, Travolta boasts just the right mixture of animal magnetism and innocence. Sort of a cross between James Dean and Rudy Kazootie.

To complement Travolta's charms, Stigwood and Carr persuaded international recording star Olivia Newton-John to make her American film debut. With more Gold records and worldwide awards than any other contemporary female vocalist, Olivia stars as Sandy, Travolta's beautifully and painfully innocent love interest. Stockard Channing, acclaimed on Broadway in "Two Gentlemen of Verona" and on film in "The Fortune," rounds out the starring roles as Rizzo, a tough-talking, very liberated "Pink Lady."

CHOREOGRAPHER

Talented and energetic Patricia Birch, a four-time Tony nominee, was selected to choreograph GREASE. Before her superb work on the film version, Pat performed the musical staging of the original Broadway production of GREASE, for which she was nominated for a Tony award. Her other three prized Tony nominations were for ''Over Here,'' starring the Andrews Sisters and featuring John Travolta, Hal Prince's ''Pacific Overtures,'' and this past year for ''Music Is . . .''

''But this (GREASE) is my first really major film commitment of this size,'' Pat explains. Ms. Birch met this new commitment by adapting her stage style to film, as she tells, ''Very simply: you let the camera spy on you. I mean, even good stage choreography doesn't leap out at you — you have to be careful that you're not falling into the proscenium. But with film, it's remembering that the audience is the eye of the camera.''

But Ms. Birch faced even more new problems with the movie version of GREASE. ''There you are with six million bucks on your back, and there are an enormous amount of musical numbers in GREASE,'' Pat says. ''Even though the essential thrust of them is somewhat the same as it was in the show, you have to use a whole different process to keep the validity of the piece.''

To achieve this validity of effect Pat came up with an unusual method for the film choreography. An unprecedented open-casting call went out on both coasts of the country and ten of the most talented dancers were selected from each coast. Barbi Alison, Carol Culver, Helena Andreyko, Dennis Daniels, Antonia Francheschi, Daniel Levans, Mimi Lieber, Sean Moran, Andy Roth, and Richard Weisman were chosen after auditions at Broadway's Lunt-Fontanne Theatre. After auditioning on a soundstage at Paramount Studios in Hollywood, Jennifer

Buchanan, Cindy DeVore, Larry Dusich, Deborah Marie Fishman, John Robert Garret, Sandy Gray, Greg Rosatti, Lou Spadaccini, Judy Susman, and Andy Tennant were selected to round out the special dancers for GREASE.

"We decided to have 20 dancers for the film and to use them throughout the movie," Pat indicates. "They became subcharacters in a sense. When you see them dancing, you should already know them. You've seen them in the classroom as well as at the hop."

On screen, D-1 through 20 (as the dancers were called on the daily sheets) may only appear to be the "background action." But on-location, it was usually the dancers who made GREASE's lavish production numbers work.

"My dancers play greasers throughout the movie," Pat says; "and they even bring those characters with them to the fantasy sequences. You almost think that they're all going to fall down — but that's the whole point. They're in character. I think we're creating another whole breed of people who can do it all."

"And then there are the numbers. In 'We Go Together' we have 150 people dancing. And its fun. I mean, how do you organize 30 of those people who you have for rehearsals, when you know you're going to add another 125. Then you get the others for one day, and they're basically extras, and it's challenging to make it all work. And it was fun, because I actually managed to get 150 people dancing together!"

THE DIRECTOR OF PHOTOGRAPHY

Bill Butler was nominated for an Academy Award for "One Flew Over the Cuckoo's Nest" in 1975. That same year he served as director of photography on "Jaws," the biggest grossing film of all time, which easily means that more people have seen his photography than any other cinematographer in film history.

Born in Colorado, Butler began his career in films working with then-novice director William Freidkin on a series of documentaries in Chicago. One of them, "The People Vs. Paul Crump," not only won the pair — the top award at the San Francisco Film Festival, it also reversed the practice of capital punishment in Chicago following its impact. Friedkin brought

Bill with him to work on his "Good Times," starring Sonny and Cher. He then worked with Jack Nicholson on "Drive, He Said," and with Francis Ford Coppola on one of his earliest features, "The Rain People." Coppola called upon Butler to photograph his critically acclaimed, Academy Award-nominated "The Conversation," and then came assignments to work with Milos Forman on "Cuckoo's Nest" and with Steven Spielberg on "Jaws."

Having started as an electronics engineer, Butler still likes to work in television where his photography for "Raid on Entebbe" and "The Execution of Private Slovak" has been appreciated by critics and public alike.

THE SCREENWRITER

Bronte Woodard arrived in Los Angeles from Atlanta on New Year's Day, 1970. He sold his first script, ''Radio Land,'' to Allan Carr for Ann-Margret, and although the project never developed, Carr and Woodard have remained good friends ever since. When Allan was looking for a screenwriter to adapt GREASE for film, Bronte received his big break.

And 1977 has been a major year for Woodard indeed. His first novel, ''Meet Me at the Melba,'' rave-reviewed in the **Los Angeles Times**, is currently up for film rights with several studios in there bidding. He is also currently adapting the best-selling ''The Lonely Lady'' to star Susan Blakely for Universal, and his ''The Bessie Smith Story'' is set to star Thelma Houston for Motown. He is also at work on screenplays for Ray Stark (''Free Style''), Allan Carr (''Open House''), and Paramount Pictures (''Ruby Red''). All of which goes to prove that his astrologist, who predicted these successes, certainly must have had a direct line to the stars.

THE COSTUME DESIGNER

Albert Wolsky has already recreated the Fifties in costumes for Bob Fosse's "Lenny," starring Dustin Hoffman, and for Paul Mazursky's "Next Stop, Greenwich Village." Born in Paris and raised in New York, Albert began as an assistant costume designer on such top Broadway musicals as "Fiddler on the Roof," "Camelot," and "I Do! I Do!" For film, he has designed the costumes for "Where's Poppa?," "Up the Sandbox," "Harry and Tonto," and "The Gambler," and this past year he worked on the critically-acclaimed "The Turning Point," starring Anne Bancroft and Shirley MacLaine, and "An Unmarried Woman," starring Jill Clayburgh and Alan Bates. His Broadway credits include "The Sunshine Boys," "All Over Town" and "Sly Fox" and his other New York stage credits include "Hamlet" in Central Park for Joseph Papp, and The Phoenix Repertory season. He was nominated for an Emmy for work on "Beauty and the Beast."

THE PRODUCTION DESIGNER

Production designer **Phillip Jefferies** began in films by setting up the screen test for Paul Newman for "The Silver Chalice." He has since worked with Newman on "Sometimes A Great Notion," "WUSA," and one of the most successful films of all time, "Butch Cassidy and the Sundance Kid." Beginning as an illustrator and later serving as assistant art director and color consultant, Jefferies was Oscar-nominated for his design for the 1974 musical version of "Tom Sawyer," for Arthur Jacobs and Readers' Digest. The following year he worked on "Huckleberry Finn" and has more recently been praised for his work on "Ode to Billy Joe." He came to GREASE having just completed work on "The Island of Dr. Moreau," starring Michael York and Burt Lancaster.